Grief
MOUNTAIN

A practical guide in recovering
from grief and loss

Mary Cranston, M.ED

Grief Mountain

A practical guide in recovering from grief and loss

Mary Cranston, M.ED

ISBN (Print Edition): 978-1-54399-480-3

ISBN (eBook Edition): 978-1-09830-874-2

I dedicate this book to my husband, Ross Praytor, and I want to thank him for comforting me as I made this hike. Ross supported me with love and encouragement. He is, in fact, the single best person I know. I love him more than my words can express, an irony for a writer, and I am genuinely amazed every day that I get to spend my life with him. Ross has been my support and consistent companion as I have traveled Grief Mountain. He has picked me up in the valleys and celebrated with me on mountain tops.

If you find yourself lost in the anguish and despair that only grief can deliver, if you are broken-hearted over a relationship that was there one day and gone the next, or if you are questioning if God has good plans for you at all –I have been there, and I understand. God made sure that I wrote this book to bring you hope and a show you there is a bright future ahead.

MC XOXO

TABLE OF CONTENTS

INTRODUCTION

My Normal Got Snatched

Why write a book on grief? I decided to write this book on a morning that I sat down to have my blissful morning coffee and personal growth time. It's a ritual I have been doing most of my adult life. But on that morning, my coffee was just too normal to engage with when my entire inner life was in a professed state of emergency. Without warning, my perfectly planned-out life was up in flames. I was experiencing, in the raw, losing the connection of the dreams that would never be.

That was a few years ago, but I can recall the memory as if it was yesterday. I must search in my past but it is there. The wound isn't throbbing with pain any longer. It's more of a disfigured scar –like a war wound. Now it's just my biography.

For a long time, even in sleep, I couldn't escape it. I would wake up feeling beat up –never refreshed. I would relive this night after night after night. And slowly the days became weeks and the weeks became months and the months became years. When I discovered Grief Mountain, I began my healing. Those painful flashbacks moved to just a memory and now they are a story in my past.

I dragged out my journal and tried to take captive the raw essence of grief. Why does grief settle into the depths of our soul? Wounding is different from hurt. Wounding settles into the morass of our soul. It's hard to capture.

Grief taught me a life lesson about what I specifically like in life. I like familiarity. I like predictability. I like being understood. I like people believing the best about me. I like having my person. I like my normal life. Grief hijacked my normal. Just gone. Abducted. It is brutal to think about it and to write about it, but I am a survivor of unpredictable circumstances that shattered and forever changed what I knew and loved about my life. There. I said it. The "truth shall set you free." That's a promise from the Almighty. Even as gloomy as it sounds, you can't help but feel a little relief.

The world around you does not skip a beat. Slowly people return to being happy and there you sit. Normal has been hijacked, sometimes by accident and sometimes on purpose. Either way, Grief is a thief. It steals your normal.

Grief knows no boundaries as it floods into every crevasse of your life. It means so many different things. I couldn't really see all of it until I was facing Grief Mountain as a devasted hiker. I wanted to pitch my tent and camp out for the rest of my life at the base of the mountain. The last thing I had the energy for was a hike. I don't even like hiking! The only hike I was interested in was the one to the store for the chocolate so I could return to my Netflix binge. The mountain looked daunting.

There's nothing we can do to disqualify grief from our lives. I wish I could remove every tear ever cried from your life and from mine. I wish I could give you back your normal, and I wish I could have my normal back. But I can't. The only thing that will spring you forward is to pursue the sweet taste of grace. And I'm talking grace-to-self. The best traveling companion over this mountain is grace. God gives us this beautiful gift called worthiness. You are enough right now. To love God is to cooperate with grace –to pull it up and put it on. Grace is the opposite of judgment and shame. It says you are doing your very best today and that is enough. Grace is letting yourself off the hook. Letting go of stringent expectations and the straight jacket you find yourself in. God created grace so that we could love ourselves and so it could accompany us over Grief Mountain. With each ache of grief, you create space for grace. For example, on a rough day when you are not able to go to work, you say, "grace-to-self" and stay home and nurture yourself and then re-evaluate work tomorrow.

Our relationship with God is individual. Like any relationship, sometimes we feel close and sometimes we feel distant. For me, grief spins me into a distant place with God. It is in these moments I see my highlight reel with God –his faithfulness and all the incredible blessings he has lavished on me throughout my life. I think of all the promises he came through for me. In the present moment of grief, I am complaining to God about how much I hate my life. But I can't escape the highlight reel of his abundant blessings. So, I wrestle in my mind if I will believe God. If I will, I trust that God sees things that I don't. Will I trust him when I don't understand? When circumstances are hard? When people betray me or reject me? When my heart is broken? Will I turn my full control over to him?

This is what I know about the character of God; he is always in my corner when I am cornered. I don't have to figure it out today. I don't have to know all the whys and why nots. All I have to do is trust. He can be trusted because the highlight reel of my past proves it over and over and over. I decide to let God sort it out. As I gaze up at Grief Mountain, I say to God, "God I want your voice to be the loudest voice in my head. Correct me, comfort me and be close to me. I trust you." It's that simple.

Your relationship with God is just that. It is yours. For me, God's goodness and love have been chasing me all the days of my life. Before God, I was chasing something in the world and was running from the stable and secure love our souls long for the most. That is an empty chase. My soul was created to be pursued and fulfilled by God's love and goodness. Long story short: God has already caught me. His goodness and love have pursued me and won me. And with that thought alone, my soul kicked in where my brain could not. I laced up my boots and put my feet on the path of trust and began my hike. I had to be brave enough to trust that God was creating an even better new normal.

CHAPTER 1

Just Get Over It?

In my lifetime I have gotten over a cold, a crush, an argument, a relationship, a bad movie. These things cause temporary misery; maybe you learn from it and you let bygones be bygones. It is a crippling mistake to think that all painful experiences can be gotten over. There are times when such a shift isn't possible. People can't always change the way they feel, think or behave simply because they want to. Grief does not work on a timeline, a framework or a checklist. Our culture today is one of impatience which is where this statement, "get over it" is derived from. "Get over it," reflects impatience, rushing and multitasking. Grief often festers in our everyday business-as-usual routines. There is no everyday life routine when loss has flipped your life upside down. When you lose a child, go through a divorce, experience suicide, lose a career, lose a pet or lose a body part there is no business as usual. The impatience that radiates in our world today unfortunately sends the message to people grieving to "get over it" quickly and "get back to your life." I think the insensitivity of "get over it" is extremely painful and wounding to our soul because it disrespects and disregards the ever-present pain we are trying to survive. And if we're honest, the people around us just want to get back to their lives. They subtly imply, hurry up with it! Be done with it already! Our world is saturated with restlessness and irritability. In addition to others sending us that message, people may push you to stop feeling the pain. But that is misguided. If the pain exists, it may make sense, because there will never come a day when you won't wish for that one moment, that one conversation or one last hello or goodbye. We also send it to ourselves. Our inner dialog can sound like, "Come on girl; get over it," "Just move on," or "What's my problem? It's been so long now." So, whether it's our voice or others, this mindset is rooted in impatience and an instant gratification social norm. This is in no way helpful to the journey of grief. All the things you have heard about getting over grief, going back to normal and moving on –they are all misrepresentations of what it means to love someone who has died. As humans, we strive for closure and resolution, but this isn't how grief rolls. Grief is like that old injury that aches when it rains. Believe it or not, grief has a significant role in our life. It becomes how we love a person despite their physical absence. Grief is an expression of love. It helps us connect to the memories. It bonds us to our shared humanity.

Long story short, I have worked in the mental health field for three decades and have sat in a confidential office with over a thousand people. Mental health can be both complex and complicated. One of the strange things about being a counselor is that no one ever sees you work, no one ever witnesses you on the job, nor do you ever get a job evaluation. Your career is done in a confidential setting. The rewarding high-value side of being a counselor/coach is that you get the privilege of being on the inside of people's lives –closely walking with them through their peaks and valleys. I am just so humbled to do this work. Every day I get to enter the world of the most courageously brave people. On most days, I float out to my car in the parking lot and whisper to myself, "Who gets to do this?" I have such a deep love for my people and am so awed by their audacity to face their challenges. The partnership with a counselor/coach and their client is so exclusive and extraordinarily different from any other relationship. What a blessed life I have had with so many remarkable people!

I feel myself giggling inside when I watch our culture get their "try-hard" on, to be individualistic, fluid, "it's all good" and "you do you" world! When it comes to grief, we are all universal, unified; we are all going to experience grief. No exceptions. We may experience it differently; however, we will all experience grief. It is one of those experiences that, for so many, are unfamiliar and frightening. Grief is strange in that you can never fully understand it until you experience it. Until that time, all a person has to go by is what they have observed and what they've been told. No one gets a pass when it comes to grief. So, we might want to invest in some hiking boots now because we will be going over Grief Mountain many times throughout our lives.

When your life has flipped, and the floodgate of feelings comes storming through, you may feel sad, angry, lonely, anxious, etc. It reminds me of taking a can of pop and vigorously shaking it and then opening it up and an overwhelming mess happens. And then we try to stuff it or minimize it so we don't become a burden to others. I am saying it now flat out –this won't work. As tempting as it is to respond with "I'm fine," don't do it. Find a therapist, mentor, counselor, coach or pastor to walk this journey with you. Find a safe place where you can process your grief and honestly say, "I'm NOT fine." Personally, I have tried to outrun, wait out, hide from and ignore it. Eventually I realized my grief wasn't going anywhere so I could either run from it forever or give in to its presence. Once the cloud of grief consumed me, it was hard to see or feel anything else. This was a holy crap moment (nothing within me wanted to visit Grief Mountain) but the only alternative was to keep running and go nowhere. In the early days of my grief, I felt like all the light had been drained from the world and everything was dark. But as the fog (acute grief) thinned, a little bit of light crept in and things started to look a little less scary and a little more manageable. Once I was able to strap up my boots, I realized this journey is made up of both good and bad. Grief grows from the same seeds of love so after someone dies, one seldom exists without the other. My greatest life lesson with grief was changing my relationship with it over time. I see it now as something nuanced, complex and beautiful as my relationships were with the people who are not here anymore. Although its ongoing presence is challenging, I embrace it because it's the source of love and connection with those who are gone.

Mindset: I must walk this journey with someone. Grief is not a solo act.

I often hear in my office: "I don't know why I can't get over this." "It has been one year, and I still feel stuck." "I should be better by now." The deal with grief is that it is impossible to estimate or put an appropriate timeline on it because it's a unique and personal journey. The recovery process and stages are the same for most people but the ability to process it is unique to the individual. No cookie cutter grief is available. Most people don't understand that grief is normal, not dysfunctional. It is also not dysfunctional to experience unpleasant grief-related thoughts and emotions from time to time years later.

Mindset: Grief has no timelines or expectations other than to keep showing up. The worst grief is ALWAYS your own. Don't compare your progress with someone else. Don't turn back or quit this journey. Keep going your way.

Grief can be an untamed giant in our life. I have personally witnessed a person's life go awry because of unresolved grief. There is no shortcut through it. It is a journey where stages of loss must be processed, released and healed –with somebody. Take all the pressure off. Let go of any expectations or timelines. Walk yourself up to the trailhead of Grief Mountain and get ready to blaze a trail and come down the other side into peace and hope.

Here's the deal with therapy, coaching or any form of personal growth. Ready? YOU HAVE TO DO THE WORK. To get up and over Grief Mountain you will need to do the work required in this book. You must claim this as your time. Your season. Your comeback. Guard your schedule and time and keep your healing a top priority, and you will exchange captivity for freedom.

Dear Hikers:

Please don't underestimate how vitally important your homework and strategizing is to your recovery. If you just read this book and put it in a drawer and never apply it, you will remain unchanged –stuck in your pain. This book is not a quick read. I want you to not move forward until your homework is completed. I share this with you in love because I have watched so many go over this mountain. The hikers that do the work gain the recovery and freedom. I will lead you through your grief and up and over this mountain; however, I can't do your homework. Welcome it and be challenged by it.

Hiking is not for the weak!

-MC xoxo

Guilt-free Journaling:

Journaling is critical to our healing and our process. And there are many ways to journal. Find which way works for you and stick with it. There are no specific guidelines for journaling so please don't guilt yourself about your homework.

Here are a few journaling strategies:

1. Combine this book and journal all over the book.

2. Purchase a journal and don't combine the book.

3. Take notes on your phone with quick notes.

4. Speak your thoughts into your phone.

5. Write long expressive sentences.

6. Make lists with bullet points.

7. Type your journaling at your computer.

Do what makes you feel comfortable, and you will feel like you are releasing it to your journal.

Getting Stronger Strategies:

1. Schedule in a personal growth time into your daily schedule. Add PG (personal growth) into your daily routine, preferably at the same time every day. My PG goes with my first cup of coffee. Every day.

2. Think on who you can walk this journey with and contact them. Set up a weekly time to meet. Ask around for a good counselor, coach or professional. Make the appointment.

3. Select which method of journaling will be best for you and prepare your journal. The purpose of journaling is to stop your mind from spinning. We can get so analytical in our thinking that we overthink everything and then get mentally paralyzed and that prevents us from taking steps forward. Through journaling we release the mind chatter on to the paper. You can write sentences, list bullet points or make lists –just do it your way. Nobody will be reading your journal. So, journal away!

My method of journaling is to mark up and write all over this book. I am also a bullet point maker and I put lots of bullets in the margins.

Now that you are ready, let's begin!

- I have my PG scheduled into my daily routine.

- I have researched and made an appointment with a coach/counselor/professional.
- I have selected my method of journaling and am ready to go to work!

1. The first step on Grief Mountain is the step of shock/numbness/disbelief. It is a large first step. Typically, when a person is going through a loss of any kind their initial response is shock. It's those first thoughts of: "this can't be happening!" "No way is this happening!" "I can't believe this is my life!" "This has to be a mistake!"

   - Journal the thoughts or questions you processed in this stage:

2. Reflect on your loss and assess whether you think you are in shock right now. If you are experiencing shock, identify it and release your feelings and thoughts into your journal. If you are no longer in the shock stage, reflect on what you can remember about the shock you experienced.

   - My current shock feels like:

   - My initial shock looked like:

3. I want to introduce you to the wrecking ball in this journey. It is called "mad & sad." Heading up the mountain you will find yourself at a dangerous trailhead called mad & sad. I call it a wrecking ball because it swings back and forth from mad to sad. Then sad to mad. This can go on for days, weeks or even months. And you

get wrecked in the process. One minute you are sad and crying. And then literally the next minute you are so mad you want to tear someone's head off. Then it's back to sad. The wrecking ball just keeps swinging back and forth. Back and forth. There is only one way to steady the wrecking ball –to stop the swing. And that is to dump all of the mad and sad thoughts from your head into your journal. Give yourself permission to unload without a filter of EVERYTHING you are mad and sad about. No guardrails, no guilt, just the truth and the mad & sad you are experiencing this day.

- Today I feel mad:

Example: "Today I am mad because this part of my life is over. I feel like everyone else is moving on with their lives."

- Today I feel sad:

Example: "Today I am really sad that you are not here to experience life with me. I am sad that I find myself in this place."

Congratulations. You have put your foot on the path to healing. You have started your trip up Grief Mountain.

It's time to self assess.

Where are you today on Grief Mountain?

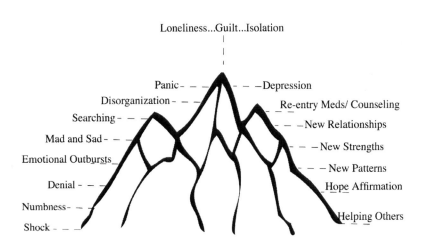

Loneliness...Guilt...Isolation

Panic - – – – – –Depression
Disorganization - – – – Re-entry Meds/ Counseling
Searching - – – – – –New Relationships
Mad and Sad - – – – – –New Strengths
Emotional Outbursts – – –New Patterns
Denial - – – Hope Affirmation
Numbness- – Helping Others
Shock - – –

CHAPTER 2

Refueling is False

The reason refueling doesn't work is because you are not ready to refuel. You are not physically, emotionally or psychologically ready for what's coming. Grief is a courageous journey. After the loss of a loved one, you must thoroughly experience all the feelings evoked by your loss and if you don't, problems and symptoms of unsuccessful grief will occur. Honestly, one of the greatest gifts God gives us is denial at the beginning of the grief journey to help us prepare, brace and cushion ourselves for the intensity of this climb up Grief Mountain. It IS INTENSE. Denial is an extremely important component to our healing. It protects your mind and you from more pain. It is normal to not fully grasp that a loved one is gone. Your mind is not ready to comprehend a life without that person. Take some baby steps toward seeing some reminders about your loved one, but do this slowly and gently. It may be a smell of cologne, a song or a photo. Cry freely. Guilt-free crying is a must. So, cry when you feel like it and don't feel guilty when you don't feel like crying. A good professional will ease you through the denial and help you move up the mountain. But for now, your denial is normal.

I am a positive girl by nature, so it bothers me that the titles of the chapters are about what doesn't work with grief. However, I must go there because there is so much wrong information and misunderstanding about grief. To get on the other side of the mountain and to heal, we just need to educate ourselves on what hinders healing. I just don't want you to waste another minute on what doesn't work. People who tell you that you are in denial or you need to snap out of it are misinformed and insensitive. Guard your heart and soul from these types of people.

Loss brings uninvited pain into our lives, but by opening yourself to the pain of your loss, in acknowledging the inevitability of the pain, you will be willing to courageously honor the pain and what is happening to you. You can plan for loss, but loss does not always comply with you! You think you have prepared and then grief hits you like a sneaker wave. It can knock you off your feet. You intellectually understand it, yet the emotional waves are hard to see coming. The word express means to press or squeeze out, to make known and reveal. Self-expression can change you and the way you perceive and experience the world. Processing your thoughts and feelings into words gives them new shape and meaning. And as you get back up and wipe the sand off your face, you start to feel like you will never be okay again. Your experience with grief is unique. Even though it may include states others experience, it is a highly individual experience. And there's no perfect way to grieve. How you grieve depends on many factors including your personality, copying style, life experiences, your faith and how significant the loss was to you.

I think one of the strangest things about death and loss is how uncomfortable it makes other people feel. People are awkward and say stupid and hurtful things sometimes. People will tell you things that are not true about your grief.

Grief does not come in five clean stages –it is messy, confusing and makes you feel like you are crazy. You grieve a person's past, present and future. Grief triggers are everywhere, like an unending display of fireworks.

The aftershock losses include the loss of self –your identity, meaning, purpose, values and trust. It is normal to question your faith. The grief process is not only about grieving the loss, but it is about getting to know yourself as a different person. You may find yourself in a new identity.

There's no normal when it comes to grieving. It gets worse before it gets better. Again, any grief is a valid loss; set boundaries with people who try to tell you differently. Put up a stiff arm to minimizing your grief. Minimizing loss is dishonoring it. Bravery is daring and doing. Courage is friendly and welcoming. Embrace courage. Cultivate a relationship with it every day, and each morning welcome it. Before you rise, say your favorite scripture or quote out loud. Look for simple ways to give voice to courage throughout the day.

This concept of refueling and just getting away from the business of our lives may be great self-care but it will not lead to healing from grief. It disrespects the natural phase of denial. Many people have told me that they went on this awesome get-a-way retreat but when they returned, there it was! Grief is ever present. You go to bed with it and you wake up with it. You have coffee with it and go to work with it. There can be many, many attempts to refuel and then you are haunted once again by grief.

Along with refueling, the concept that time heals just isn't a thing. I know firsthand it isn't true. I am not sure who made that up, but this is how I know that it is false. Over the past 20 years I have had a large number of clients tell me about a significant loss. And then I ask them, "So when did this take place?" And they will answer, "Fifteen years ago." They have been trying to refuel and recover from grief for fifteen years and they are honestly back at the very first step on Grief Mountain.

Mindset: Time does not heal grief. Persistent courage and persistent hard work heals grief. Your willingness to honestly affirm your need for mourning will help you survive this excruciating time in your life.

Sometimes people try to refuel by just praying. And as powerful as God Almighty is, he also gave us professionals and trusted people to walk this journey with. The funny thing about grief is that some of our otherwise healthy ways of refueling just don't work for grief. Recently I had been going through a significant grief issue and using refueling attempts like: a weekend away, talking it through with a friend and my pastor, reading books on grief, having a spa day, taking vitamins, etc. I wanted to shout it from the mountaintop, "I can't shake this ever-present grief. Nothing works." And as I stood on the top of that mountain shaking my fist, I realized I was on the wrong journey and definitely the wrong mountain. The pain of grief will keep trying to get your attention until you unleash your courage to slowly, gently and in small doses open yourself up to its presence. If you do not acknowledge your grief, it will consume you.

I have learned that the pain surrounding the closed heart of grief is the pain of living against yourself, the pain of denying how the loss changes you. Instead of dying while you are alive, you can choose to allow yourself to remain open to the pain, which in large part honors the love you feel for the person who has died. After all, love and grief are two sides of the same precious coin.

Mindset: Embrace the denial and search. Then find a professional who can help. Work hard. Decide that you will not let this grief tank you.

Growing Stronger Strategies:

1. Do a self-assessment. Review Grief Mountain. If you feel like you are no longer in shock/numbness/disbelief then you are ready for your next step up the mountain. If you are still dealing with shock/

numbness/disbelief, go back and continue to repeat the homework from the last chapter. Repeat it daily until you are out of that stage.

2. The next step up the mountain is emotional outbursts. This step is an uncomfortable and an unsettling step. Personally, it just makes my insides cringe. However, you have got to do it! You cannot skip this stage or you will be forever stuck.

   • Reflect on your emotional outbursts for the day. Journal on the emotional outbursts:

   • Journal- I will not always feel the way I do today because:

   • Journal- I am doing okay now. Grief will not destroy me because:

   • Journal- I will make it through this experience, just as others have before me. Who comes to mind that made it through terrible grief?

3. Here is the key to this step and to turning the corner on grief. We need to let our feelings out. Give yourself permission to let all feelings, all feelings, all feelings bubble up to the top and bubble out of you. Trying to squelch them, sweep them under or sit on them will only grow them. They will come bursting out of you at the most awkward times –trust me.

- Journal- Today my feelings bubbled up and I let them out and then I felt them.

- Why is it so hard to release my feelings?

4. Identify the best place for you to have emotional outlets. Get in front of this by giving yourself permission, and then find a place to let feelings flow. My favorite places to let my emotions out are in my car, in my bed or in my favorite chair.

  - My emotional release place will be:

5. Unexpected outbursts require that you have an exit plan. For example, put a timeline on things. When you are going to a social event and you don't know how you will handle it, or if you will make it –have an exit plan. Have a reason you must leave. Be upfront about your timeline. Tell people when you must take off.

  - Journal your exit plan:

6. Complete emotional surprise! This is when you had no clue that your emotions would suddenly pop up. Give yourself permission to pause, pray and push through. You don't have to explain anything to anybody. Don't try to analyze what is happening and explain it. You

already know it is a part of Grief Mountain and it is an emotional outburst; all you need to do is pause, pray and push through.

- Journal on your latest emotional surprise:

_____

Mindset: The emotions you need to feel and process are the exact same emotions you are doing everything you can to avoid. Choose grief. Cry when you need to. Call when you need to. Feel overwhelmed when you need to. In exchange, you will find the hope, courage and desire to once again live a full and rewarding life.

_____

7. The important part of this stage is the release. If you want to move through this stage and continue your hike up the mountain, use this release tool.

Tool: Every time you identify a feeling you say:

"I FEEL _____ AND I JUST DO."

This tool allows you to release it out. Do not analyze, explain or pick apart your feeling. Just say out loud: "I feel _____ and I just do." Done.

- Journal how many times today you said, "I feel _____ and I just do."

Record:

Analyzing our feelings to death can paralyze us from the release as well as forward progress. Here's the deal with feelings –they are unpredictable, fickle and in a constant state of change. Don't empower them; don't let them lead your life because they will lead you right off the mountain back to the depths of despair. Say this statement when you are driving in your car, at home, anywhere. You will experience instant relief.

Mindful: I feel _____ and I just do.

8. Journal the grief potholes of emotional outbursts. Every time you have an emotional outburst, journal about it and how you identified the feeling and used the tool:

"I feel _____ and I just do."

9. Journal and tackle the wrecking ball of mad & sad.

- Today I feel mad:

- Today I feel sad:

It's time to self assess.

Where are you today on Grief Mountain?

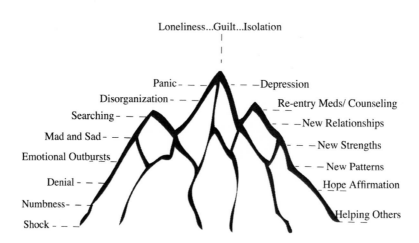

Loneliness...Guilt...Isolation

Panic — — — —Depression

Disorganization - — — Re-entry Meds/ Counseling

Searching - — — — —New Relationships

Mad and Sad - — — — New Strengths

Emotional Outbursts — — — New Patterns

Denial - — Hope Affirmation

Numbness- — Helping Others

Shock - — —

CHAPTER 3

Ending the Unending Search

All good searches usually come to an end, eventually! We all do it.

We lose our keys, our phone, our glasses, but typically we find them or we replace them. Searching in the grief process leads to nowhere. It's a dead end every time. Our search is looking for reasons, explanations, rational truths, direction, causes and truths to make sense of the tragedy. And then we pick up the search the next day. Day after day.

It is through dealing with the pain that spurs learning and growing. An aspect of dealing with pain is facing the endless "what if" thoughts. It is dealing with these thoughts that you find a way to forgive yourself and discover what is meaningful to you. As the meaning evolves, you question all of the previous life altering decisions and begin to make major life changes such as what you do and how you spend your time. What was once important may no longer be important. This can sometimes confuse the people around you.

You know you are at the search phase of the mountain if you hear your thoughts say, "But maybe," or "What if?" Searching for answers and facts act as a defense and help us block the waves of pain. The search phase is a healthy part of grief because it can cushion the pain that is coming to the psyche. It means we are still dealing with the denial shock and the reality is too much for the psyche to handle. Denial, shock and searching help us cope and make survival possible. There is grace in denial. It is nature's way of letting in only as much as you can handle. Embrace the search. As you ask yourself the questions, you are beginning the healing process. You are becoming stronger and your denial is fading. The feelings you were denying are starting to surface because you are more ready now. It is so important to be patient at this point of your climb. Don't pressure yourself with expectations. Accept that you need to experience your pain, your emotions and your own way of healing –all in your own timing. Don't judge or compare yourself to others; remember that no one else can tell you how you should mourn.

Accompanied with the search can come disorganization and denial. The search can become all-consuming, so it can produce disorganization and forgetfulness and a little denial. So just know you are normal if you are finding yourself forgetful and disorganized because your brain is on overload. Give yourself lots of grace and self-love as you are doing your best!

Please know that the search is normal, healthy and an important part of your healing. Let the search happen. Give yourself permission to go there, get out your magnifying glass and explore all the facts –big facts and little facts and all that's in-between.

As you are standing on Grief Mountain, in the search position, it is that stage that begins to equal out your feeling life and your thinking life. They collide at the search phase and that ultimately helps us in our healing. Thinking and feeling begin to team up together which gives us power to get up and over this mountain.

Eventually the search phase will run its course. We exhaust ourselves and are imprisoned with our unending questions and research. And then finally we find ourselves standing alone at the end of a dead-end street. And it is there that we realize none of our questions, searching and researching will bring about any change. We come face to face with our reality that even if we were to receive the answers to our questions, we would remain sad and lost in our grief.

Mindset: Feelings and Thinking make a powerful team. Embrace the search.

Grow Strong Strategies:

1. Journal (3-4 times a week) on your search progress. Draw a line down the middle of your paper and title the left side with

"Maybe" and the right side with "Truth."

Release all the maybes and then later come back and add the truths.

- No matter how ridiculous the search may seem or how crazy some of your maybes turn out –dump them all into your journal. All of them!

Maybe: Truth:

2. As always you want to share your search with a professional when you think you have come to the end of the search.

Journal and prepare to share with your professional:

3. Journal and tackle the wrecking ball. (7 journal entries).

Today I am mad…. _____

Today I am sad…. _____

Today I am mad_____

Today I am sad_____

Today I am mad _____

Today I am sad _____

Today I am mad _____

Today I am sad _____

Today I am mad _____

Today I am sad _____

Today I am mad _____

Today I am sad _____

Today I am mad _____

Today I am sad _____

Dear Hikers:

Remember: do not go on to the next chapter until you have completed your homework. This hike is not a sprint. It is a slow and steady pace that leads to recovery.

MC

It's time to self assess.

Where are you today on Grief Mountain?

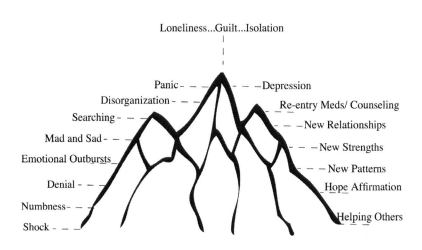

Loneliness...Guilt...Isolation

Panic — — — — — Depression

Disorganization — — — Re-entry Meds/ Counseling

Searching — — — — New Relationships

Mad and Sad — — — — New Strengths

Emotional Outbursts — — New Patterns

Denial — — Hope Affirmation

Numbness — — Helping Others

Shock — — —

CHAPTER 4

The Wrecking Ball

We are at the most dangerous part of our hike. There is a wrecking ball attached to a million-ton tree trunk that swings back and forth. This wrecking ball is called mad & sad and its purpose is to knock you off the trail and send you free falling down the mountain. Being mad is a normal and healthy part of experiencing loss. It is when you find yourself blaming and lashing out in anger. The anger can be directed at many things and many people. We feel guilty for being angry which in turn makes us angrier. Then we may just be spewing anger everywhere –at strangers, doctors, loved ones, God, innate objects. And finally, and most critical, you may be angry with yourself. You may be guilting yourself for not being able to save the person or the situation. It is not uncommon to go through a spiritual crisis. Family and close friends are sometimes taken aback or offended by the anger because it can surface just as you are beginning to function again. You can't fix this for other people. Don't put your energy there. Keep addressing the wrecking ball in your journal and eventually the anger will soften and leave altogether. Anger is a natural part of loss.

People tell us to reach out to God but sometimes we are too angry. That's okay because God can handle our anger. People will tell us to call them but what do they know? We feel resentful. We are too ticked off to reach out. Anger plays a large role in grief and loss. It colors the grieving by pushing others away, making excuses for behavior and withdrawing to avoid pain. I have found from sitting with many people that for the majority, anger is easier and more acceptable than being sad. Sad comes from hurt and we don't want to hurt anymore. We fear exposing our vulnerability, so we lash out at those around us. It could be towards someone close or a total stranger. It's scary if you've been a "nice girl" all your life and then suddenly you're an emotional "rager girl." Anger is your body's natural reaction to threat. The threat can be real or perceived. Someone died; there's nothing more threatening. There is nothing wrong with anger. When we let it out, we are often misperceived. When people tell you to just "let it out," they are not thinking about the anger or the meltdown. They are thinking of a gentle cry. So, when anger shows up loudly, they are confused and perplexed.

Meanwhile, your emotions bob up and down and it's scary because you feel so unstable. Grace-to -self. You are coming to terms with your new normal. Remember that when normal people go through abnormal events, they tend to act abnormal. Here's the catch. Anger is normal on Grief Mountain, but you want to use it to fuel you up the mountain in a constructive way rather than sliding down the mountain in a destructive way.

The thing to remember is that mad & sad cannot creep into our new normal. A permanent mad & sad does not work. To get up and over this crevasse on our hike is to recognize that you are not yourself (grace-to-self). Practice grace with yourself and others. The only way to let go of anger is to ask for and to grant forgiveness. Forgiveness is your free pass out of prison.

The wrecking ball can swing in your life forever if you are not intentional about processing it through, journaling and moving on. Mad & sad have the potential to steal your joy, peace and your vey life. If you start hearing comments like, "They just never recovered," "They just aren't the same person," "Part of them died that day." I say this with complete sensitivity: As horrific and devastating as grief and loss can be, we must acknowledge that other people still need us. We still have a purpose on this earth, so we need to do something purposeful with this tragedy. Someday, possibly, you can help someone else with grief. Personally, I can't have my losses be for nothing; I refuse to let that happen.

Mad & sad are very efficient at rocking us off kilter and ruining our days. They are so powerful that they can lead us into thinking we may be crazy! The crazy cycle of mad & sad is like a wrecking ball that swings back and forth –back and forth in your mind and in your emotions all day long. One minute you are sad and in tears and the next minute you are so angry and bitter. Hence you feel crazy! Like I use to say to my three children when I really, really needed them to hear me: "Can I please have your eyes?" And once they looked at my eyes, I would proceed. So, Hiker…can I please have your eyes? Hear this clearly. YOU ARE NOT CRAZY. You are normal. You are processing a difficult stage of grief. Everyone who has experienced loss also experiences the wrecking ball of mad & sad. Hang in there. Stay persistent and do the work.

Mindset: I am determined to face the mad & sad wrecking ball in my life. Deal with it. Shut it down and not allow it to take me out.

Grow Strong Strategies:

Here we go again. Our goal is to dump all of the mad & sad out of your entire being, Dump away! Make a daily journal entry that begins with these two prompts:

Today I am sad:

Today I am mad: i.e. Today I am sad because I can't call my husband and tell him my exciting news.

I.e. Today I am mad that I ran out of time with my husband. I have been robbed.

Do the work today so that you can be free in the future.

- Reflect and journal on- Grief is very personal and is something that you do (not something that happens to you); the one who is ultimately in charge of it is you.

- Journal- What did you do today to take charge of your grief?

- Often at this stage of grief you just feel completely robbed. Robbed of your present and of your future.

- Journal and describe how you feel robbed and ripped off by your loss:

- The challenge with grief is getting back up- again.

- Journal and share a time this week when you didn't want to get back up and keep going, but you did it anyway:

It's time to self assess.

Where are you today on Grief Mountain?

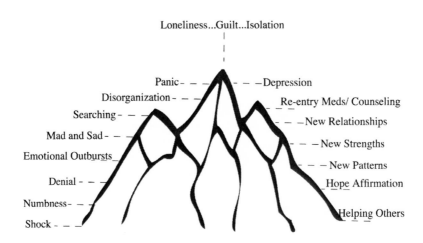

Loneliness...Guilt...Isolation

Panic - — — - — — —Depression

Disorganization - — —   — _Re-entry Meds/ Counseling

Searching - —   - — —New Relationships

Mad and Sad - —   - — —New Strengths

Emotional Outbursts   - — — New Patterns

Denial - —   Hope Affirmation

Numbness- —   Helping Others

Shock - — —

CHAPTER 5

No One Escapes a Little Hypothermia on Grief Mountain

At the peak of Grief Mountain is where the hypothermia lingers. Hypothermia is a condition in which the body's core temperature drops below 95 degrees. It is the number one killer of outdoor recreation and the number one killer in our trip across Grief Mountain. At the very top of Grief Mountain is isolation-guilt-loneliness. Like hypothermia, isolation-guilt-loneliness are often unrecognizable killers for elderly, homeless, addicts, parents who lose a child, devastating divorces and death. It is so painful it can derail a total life –sometimes forever. That is not going to be you.

With hypothermia it is crucial to know how to prevent a life-threatening loss of body heat and how to recognize the symptoms and safely reverse them. In the exact same way, it is critical to identify the peak of the mountain and be alert to symptoms of intense grief and reverse them.

God created people to be warm-blooded with the capability of generating their own body heat –unless something goes wrong. When the body begins to lose heat faster than it can be produced, the risk of hypothermia sets in. Even a drop of two to three degrees can have devastating consequences. In the same way, God created counselors, coaches, pastors and helpers to come along side of us when we are standing all alone on the peak of Grief

Mountain. Grief is not a journey that was designed for traveling alone. Being alone intensifies the grief and makes it unbearable.

Wet clothes, brisk wind, fatigue and hunger are all symptoms that lead to hypothermia. Once the hypothermia sets in, you will see violent shaking, pale and cold skin, lack of coordination and decreased mental activity.

While standing on the most dangerous place of Grief Mountain, be aware of these symptoms: difficulty concentrating, chronic tiredness, preoccupation of death and a sense of disbelief regarding the loss long after it has occurred. Although these symptoms are normal for anyone going through grief, it is when they turn into a permanent stage that the hypothermia-like dysfunctions set in and take over the mental health.

How do you know that the hypothermia-type of grief is lingering around? It could look like:

- You are very uncomfortable outside of your home and you resist attending anything.

- You have fallen into making excuses to not participate in any thing –keeping people at bay.

- Being tired is your constant companion. You never experience relief from being tired.

- Absence of self-care. Not wanting to shower or do your normal hygiene.

- Loss of interest in things you have always enjoyed in the past.

- Wanting to stay in bed all day.

- Eating all day or starving all day –extreme eating patterns.

- Dark. Dark. Dark thoughts.

So…Grief Travelers…if these have set in and you are starting to get the shakes of hypothermia, don't panic. You are about to leave the peak of Grief

Mountain and begin your descent down the other side and personal growth and peace are waiting for you. But first let's do our work!

Self-care will be a ritual for you as you hike this treacherous mountain. We will do self-care from now until forever. People forget how stressful grief is on the mind, body and soul. Grief is extremely stressful. Typically, we are able to handle our everyday stressors but when grief/loss show up, we need to super-size our self-care because grief depletes our physical and emotional coping mechanisms. Learning to manage grief and stress can help you in all areas of your life and health. It can make you feel better spiritually, mentally, physically and relationally. The mental health benefits are exuberant. Self-care may feel a little selfish or odd at the beginning. Our best mental health is when we are living a balanced life. Well, there is nothing balanced about grief and this hike over Grief Mountain. We have to combat the stress with self-care. It's a must! Yet, once you start to feel and experience the health benefits you will be a believer.

Grow Strong Strategies:

1. **Self-Care Survival Strategy:**

   - Pull together a healthy food plan that can work for now. Remember the brain is an organ and it needs protein and specific nutrients to nurse it back to health.

   - My food plan will be _____

   - Just move. Again, the brain is an organ, so we need to move it.

My exercise plan will be_____

   - Learn one new thing every day. This has never been easier. Just push a button on YouTube, the Internet or the TV.

My one new thing to learn will be_____

- Be on the lookout for self-medicating through binging on: alcohol, weed, food, prescription medication, TV, shopping online, etc. Self-medication can grow into a bigger problem than the current grief you are facing. This can be sneaky and hard to spot sometimes.

Am I aware of any self-medicating going on right now? _____

- Develop a sleep routine. Determine a set time to go to bed and a set time to get up every day. Try super hard to not deviate from it. My sleep routine is:

  - All electronics turned off at 8:30 pm.

  - Chill time and a little trash TV or prep for the next day.

  - Hot cleanse bath and book at 9:30 pm.

  - Do final pm hygiene and take melatonin at 10:30 pm.

  - Lights out. I will not get out of bed again. If I can't sleep, I listen to my Netflix show until I snooze off.

My sleep routine will be _____

- Try to have extra time with your pet or a friend's pet.

I will put pet time into my schedule _____

Pamper yourself with a beauty treatment that you don't typically do (men you can do this too!)

My pampering for the week is _____

2. **Isolation Prevention Plan**

Isolation can be deadly on Grief Mountain. It is not a solo hike.

- Choose one trusted, comfortable friend who knows you well and set up a standing date with them. It could be coffee on Saturday mornings or pizza on Friday nights or a Sunday night phone call. The key is the standing date, every week, no matter what. You need to put yourself out there to add someone else's thoughts. Perspectives and wisdom top your own.

My trusted friend is _____ and our standing date is _____

- Remember that isolation is the enemy's playground. This is where he can take up space in our mind. Refuse to give this to him. Limit your alone time no matter how much you want it.

- Embrace input in your home and avoid quietness. Play music, an interesting TV channel, Alexa music, YouTube teachings, radio, podcasts –anything but quiet.

My home engagement will be _____

- Push yourself to have one outing a day. It may be to the store, mall, library or just getting some good coffee and going for a drive. Move your brain; it is a host for your emotions. Move. Put yourself in a different environment. Baby steps all the way. Just move.

- My daily outing will be_____

- Make sure you have your broken record packed and ready to play if you run into anyone you want to avoid. You will not be anxious or need to avoid them because you already know what you are going to say. Your broken record.

My broken record is:

3.

4. **Guilt Busting Survival Strategy:**

- It is time to turn the page to guilty feelings and put that book on the shelf. Not one thought or emotion will change your current situation. It is time to say goodbye to guilt. Guilt will rob you and keep you sedentary and block your steps forward.

  - My plan to eliminate guilt self-talk is:

- Be honest with yourself. If you continue to camp out on the top of Grief Mountain where guilt grows, you risk never coming down the other side. The healthy side that recovers and moves forward. Pull up your guilt stake and chuck it as far as you can from the top of the mountain and replace it with grace. You are doing the best you can. And that is enough.

- Thought replacement. Dive into God's word and find all the scriptures on grace. Look for motivational quotes and inspiration. Every time you have a guilty thought, replace it with a grace scripture. Nothing will get you off the peak of Grief Mountain like God's word. Find it and activate it in your mind.

I am recording my positive scripture and quotes:

Dear Hikers,

I can hear you, dear travelers, pulling up your stakes and closing out this campsite and taking steps forward coming down the other side. I am cheering you on!

It's time to self assess.

Where are you today on Grief Mountain?

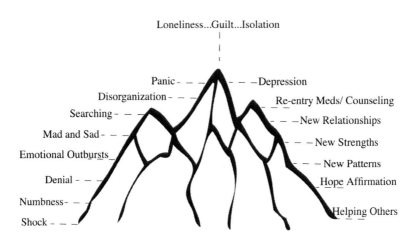

Loneliness...Guilt...Isolation

Panic - — — - - —Depression

Disorganization - — — Re-entry Meds/ Counseling

Searching - — - - —New Relationships

Mad and Sad - — - - — New Strengths

Emotional Outbursts - - — New Patterns

Denial - — Hope Affirmation

Numbness - — Helping Others

Shock - — —

CHAPTER 6

Side Stepping Grief Is an Off-Kilter Dance

After 20 years in my profession, it is my opinion that very few people escape situational depression, especially in the world we live in! Not to sound like an old person but the chaos, stress, anxiety and violence that we experience on a daily basis are at the core of situational depression. There are many types of depression (clinical/ bipolar). If you feel better calling it the blues –that works too. Call it what you want; however, as human beings we all face situations we are not able to pull ourselves out of. So, in order to come down the other side of Grief Mountain into the beautiful wild flowers and meadows we have to take an honest look at ourselves and situational depression.

The first big stride coming off the peak and descending the other side is that we have to realize the toll that the climb up the mountain has taken on our brain. The grief journey is constant. Grief seems to be your new BFF. You can't escape it. We wake up with it, go to bed with it and experience it all throughout our day. It is the constant companion we wish we could lose. Because of its persistence, our brain does not get a lot of rest or restoration. The brain is fatigued; this drains an important chemical, serotonin, from our brain, so it is running on fumes. It is at this point we need to push ourselves to go get an assessment for depression and talk to a professional. Then, follow the professional's directions. Every person is different; however, if you need an antidepressant to refuel your brain at this point of your journey, just know it may enable you to stay the course. Situational depression is just that. It's for a situation or a season. When you get off Grief Mountain you will probably not need the medication any longer.

The second big stride forward is to take an open and honest look in the mirror. See if hopelessness and despair are ever present. This is where grief and depression can collide. The grief develops into situational depression. The grief journey is a long taxing journey and it can be difficult on the body and the brain.

What does situational depression look like?

- Fatigue or loss of energy almost every day.

- Feelings of worthlessness or guilt almost every day.

- Impaired concentration or indecisiveness.

- Diminished interest or pleasure in almost all activities nearly every day.

- Restlessness or feeling slowed down.

- Random thoughts of suicide.

- Significant weight loss or gain.

The third big stride forward is getting professional help. You may need a coach or a counselor for this situation or season. I have sat with over a thousand people in my career and I can tell you from my chair that grief is not a solo journey. It is a journey that should be shared and walked through with another person. You will try to talk yourself out of this over and over. Don't fight this. Just do it. Ask a trusted friend or your doctor for a referral. The sooner you get started the sooner you get healed.

Grow Strong Strategies:

1. Make an appointment with your doctor and discuss your situation and a depression assessment.

- My doctor's appointment is scheduled for:

2. Make a counseling/coach appointment and begin your work.

   - My counseling appointment is scheduled for:

3. Make a list of questions for your counselor/coach to make sure they will provide: tools, strategies, books and practical application.

- My questions for my coach/counselor are:

4. At this point in the book we are going to hit the pause button. As you are getting your professional appointments lined up, we are going to go back to chapter 1 and review each chapter and make sure we are still using and applying what we have learned so far.

Remember that the hike up Grief Mountain can be a slippery slope sometimes. You may be striding forward and then all of a sudden you have slid back down the mountain to mad & sad again. Go pack and review your tools and strategies. Reactivate them if needed.

- What tools and strategies do I need to remember most right now:

5. The final big stride at this point of the hike is to take a break; it can also be helpful to step away from your grief and out of your head. Go on a short trip, take an unexpected day adventure or talk to someone new. These things bring time and distance and widen

our perspective and that helps taper grief. To move forward and avoid hypothermia, be honest with yourself and avoid hiding in your grief. This creates a victim mindset and keeps your victory mindset further away. Embracing your circumstances is the first step to move beyond your current state. It doesn't mean you like what is happening; instead, you accept that it's taking place through you. In a weird way, you can welcome your circumstances instead of expecting them to resolve all on their own. They seldom do, until you examine your actions and find a solution. A poor solution is better than running away from the pain because at the very least, it's a starting point towards coming down the other side of the mountain. Spiritual intervention and self-empowerment team together to fend off their hypothermia and redirect our steps.

- What spiritual habits, rituals or routines can I add to my daily schedule?

It's time to self assess.

Where are you today on Grief Mountain?

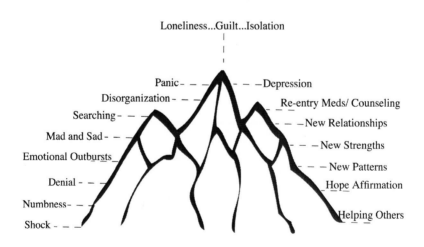

Loneliness...Guilt...Isolation

Panic — Depression

Disorganization — Re-entry Meds/ Counseling

Searching — New Relationships

Mad and Sad — New Strengths

Emotional Outbursts — New Patterns

Denial — Hope Affirmation

Numbness — Helping Others

Shock —

CHAPTER 7

New Patterns Are Showing Up

This is such an important moment in our journey. This is the place where all of a sudden you get a glimpse of some new fresh energy. Not a lot! But a little. And a little is huge. If you are doing the work that this book requires, you cannot help but to be developing new thoughts, managing emotions, getting professional help, and doing self-care. THESE ARE ALL NEW PATTERNS!! And guess what new patterns lead to? A new normal.

If you have had a chance to bump into a fellow hiker who has climbed Grief Mountain, you will discover that they have conquered grief and sound like people who have done such intriguing and precarious things. They will tell you not so much about what they have lost, but more so about what they have unlocked. Their lives will not be lived only in memories of the past, but also in plans for the future. You might be asking yourself right now, "Is she serious?" I reassure you –if you work through grief in the ways I have been assigning you to do, you will not only think of new things, but in time, you will sound like an adventurous hiker!

Decision making is one of the most problematic challenges you will face as you work at recovering your balance and creating new patterns for your new normal. Although the numbness, shock, and denial have worn off, making any decision takes major effort. And at first the decisions come flooding in: paperwork, assets, routine changes, etc. But now decision making takes on a new magnitude. The pressure is new because it shifts from what you need to do/accomplish to –what do you want to do? You hear a still small voice say, "It's time to move on." Your challenge is motivation. Therefore, deciding on the following three patterns will get your feet on the right path. Motivation starts with healthy patterns.

If this feels super slow to you, you know what to do. Give yourself grace because healing happens gradually; it can't be forced or hurried and there is no normal timeline. Some people plot over Grief Mountain and others take two strides forward and three strides backwards. Whatever your grief experience, it's important to be patient with yourself and to allow the process to unfold. Eventually you will get a glimpse of sunshine and some new patterns will arrive.

Let's look at patterns starting from the inside out. The pattern or habit of self-care will formulate new energy –starting with your sleep. Stick with your sleep routine at all costs. The sleep routine must be a non-negotiable in your life. The grief journey is so draining mentally, emotionally and physically. Sleep is the one time we can experience a break from our loss. Nurture this new pattern.

The pattern of hygiene is a critical new pattern to sustain. It sounds kind of silly, yet daily hygiene just makes us feel fresh and more energetic. The old saying, "you look good, you feel good," has a thread of truth to it. Whatever your hygiene routine is –keep it going!

My hygiene routine looks like:

- Take a long shower

- Do my skin care routine in the shower

- Moisturize

- Brush my teeth

- Do my hair, even if it is throwing it up in a ponytail with a baseball hat

- Day time make up, at least a little lipstick

- Get dressed and go!

In the early stages of grief, I could not do this hygiene routine. The last thing I wanted to do was take a shower. It was just too overwhelming.

Try to do some form of this every day. It seems basic but when you are in the middle of grief even the most basic task is a challenge. Your hygiene routine will formulate into a new pattern that will battle your blues on a daily basis.

The third critical pattern at this point is your standing date with a friend. This pattern will not only bring joy and fulfillment into your life, it will be a life-giving pattern. It will honestly keep you off the peak of Grief Mountain as it keeps isolation and loneliness at bay. Because we are ready to embrace life again, as healing takes its erratic and eccentric course, all we can ask is for others to be near. This is a vulnerable but necessary ask. Find a trusted friend that you can express your needs to, maybe just to show up and be near. What we ask of friends in bereavement is warmth. We need friends when we think that all we have is ash. Friends can help us know that it is not dust that remains, but new growth will appear once more. Friends are essential in our grief because death makes us feel alone and exposed. And it is never safe to hike alone. Fellow hikers help us to maintain closeness to others, without words, so that loneliness is a temporary state.

My hope for you is that at this point of your journey these three habits are evolving into healthy patterns in your life. If they are not quite there yet, go back and rededicate yourself to them until they become a pattern. As I have repeatedly said, no two people grieve the same way. The way we think and feel, the way our body functions and the way we interact with others may all be affected; no matter what our intense experiences with grief may be, they are temporary. There is life after grief. The first sign of new life is a new pattern.

Grow Strong Strategies:

1. Write down and post your sleep routine in a visible place so you frequently see it and can master it.

Journal- My new sleep routine includes:

2. Write down and post your hygiene routine in the bathroom so you can consistently follow it.

- My new hygiene routine includes:

- Write down your friend and standing date:

3. If you are struggling with these three patterns, reach out and find accountability. Ask your trusted friend or therapist to hold you accountable to doing these three life-changing habits.

- Journal- I will ask for help from:

  - New Patterns:
  - Sleep Routine
  - Hygiene Routine
  - Friend Date routine

It's time to self assess.

Where are you today on Grief Mountain?

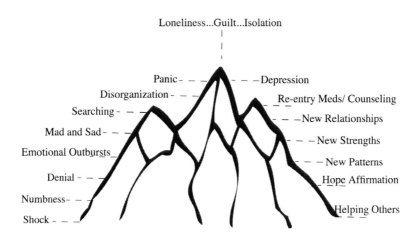

Loneliness...Guilt...Isolation

Panic - — — - — — —Depression

Disorganization - — — Re-entry Meds/ Counseling

Searching - — New Relationships

Mad and Sad - — New Strengths

Emotional Outbursts New Patterns

Denial - — Hope Affirmation

Numbness- — Helping Others

Shock - — —

CHAPTER 8

New Life Is A Choice

I am overjoyed to be at this place in this book and in our journey. As we are getting closer to the bottom of the mountain, the grass looks greener and the wildflowers look brighter! Not sure if you've noticed but as we are starting our decline down the mountain, we are no longer talking about what doesn't work. We are now at a place where we are experiencing positive change and talking about what is working. We know we will have occasional slips on the mountain and we may find ourselves in mad & sad or on the peak of isolation-guilt-loneliness. We don't have to panic if we find ourselves visiting these stages again. Remember the key word is visiting. We are not pitching our tent here. We may be on a brief visit and we need to pick up our tools and then put our feet back on the trail and keep descending this mountain.

As our new patterns take root, we will feel a little more comfortable getting out with people and in social situations. Things we use to avoid, we now feel up for. It can be as simple as going to the store or attending a family function. All of a sudden you feel the avoidance lift. It feels strange at first. You will hear yourself say, "I think I'm going to go for a little bit." It's a mind-body-soul thing. They are healing and with the healing comes energy and courage to do the things you have been avoiding.

We are very aware that nothing is the same as it was before you lost your person to death or divorce, moved to a strange city or faced the impact of a tragic injury. These tasks to be done may be the same, but you are not the same! Your energy level will be low as you return to work or full-time parenting or school. You may want an excessive amount of sleep, or face an excessive amount of sleeplessness.

Yet, there is good news. As you move beyond the first few weeks at returning to life, the absoluteness of your loss bubbles up and with that realization comes pain. It's the usual necessities of your life needing attention. You will recognize the demanding, dominating, decisions you are facing minute by minute. You must choose to live again. And making up your mind to live again means taking charge of your own grief.

As we venture out socially and relationally, it is important that you have memorized your broken record to share with non-grievers so that if anything unexpected comes up, you are prepared to respond and resist the urgency to flee –get the heck out of there! Sometimes we will get a flutter of anxiety when we begin to go out socially and re-engage with life. All of the broken records have three points and are easy to memorize. After you say your broken record it is very important to flip the conversation away from you and onto them. Our emotions get overwhelmed when people ask us too many questions. Most people truly care and have good intentions but do not realize that their questions overwhelm us. This can cause us to shut down which leads to finding the exit door and returning to isolation. The energy expended to revisit, go back and verbalize the whole thing is not a good use of your energy. Of course, with your inner circle people you give a personal update, but everyone else gets the broken record. The peace and energy that a broken record can bring to your life is priceless. The broken record is KEY to your recovery with grief.

Once you prepare your broken record, memorize it. You will feel less anxious and nervous to re-engage. There will not be any surprises because you already have prepared and memorized your response. This will free you up to be comfortable and partake in the activity.

It is crucial to remember where people are coming from who are not grieving. You need to extend grace to others and not expect them to handle your grief better than you are. You must be aware that people cannot be something other than who they are. Let them off the hook. And be mindful that most people want to help. They mean well even when they do hurtful things. And most importantly, you want to be patient with others, as you want them to be patient with you.

So, fellow Hiker. I need to pause and tell you how proud I am of you for this audacious hike. You are on the final stretch of the mountain. Stay encouraged. I do need to warn you at this point that making a decision to live again after a major loss is not easy. It requires your strength, new tools, new patterns, new mindset and flat out grit to keep moving forward. You cannot wait until you feel better and then decide to live again. You must make a decision intellectually because you know it's right, and then wait for your feelings to catch up. They will.

I want to give you total permission to take a timeout from the heaviness of grief. Give yourself escapes and let yourself fall into something that is totally mindless for you. Craft up a "Fun Things To Do" list and work your way through your list. This is healthy and refreshing and provides new energy. Remember that a fun escape is not the same thing as avoidance.

Grow Strong Strategies:

1. I want you to write out your broken record on a note card or on a quick note in your phone. The best solution is to memorize your broken record. It is a major tool in managing your grief.

   • Broken Record/Death:

Someone asks you how you are doing (with a big sad face)

Example- Your 3 step response is:

2. "Thanks for asking."

3. "I am getting some professional help and getting better."

4. "I appreciate your prayers."

FLIP IT: "How are you?" (Get the focus off you and on to them.)

Broken Record/Divorce:

Someone asks you how you are doing with the divorce: "How are the kids?" (with a big sad face)

Example- Your 3-step response is:

1. "I appreciate your concern."

2. "As tough as it was…it's for the best."

3. "My kids are getting professional help and are very resilient."

FLIP IT: "How are things at work going? (Get the focus off you and onto them.)

• Broken Record/Loss of a child:

Someone asks you how you are doing? (with a big sad face)

Example- Your 3-step response is:

1. "Definity my hardest journey ever."

2. "I am getting professional help and getting better each day."

3. "I appreciate your prayers and concerns."

FLIP IT: "How are you?"

• Broken Record/Job Loss:

Someone says: "I am so sorry to hear about your job. How are you doing?" (with a big sad face)

Example- Your 3-step response is:

1. "Thanks for asking."

2. "Honestly it has been quite the challenge."

3. "I am hopeful and have some things on the horizon."

FLIP IT: "What's new with you?"

Broken Record/Illness:

Someone says: "I am really sorry to hear about your illness. How is it going?" (with a big sad face)

Example- Your 3-step response is:

1. "I appreciate your concern."

2. "It's extremely challenging."

3. "I am hopeful- continue to pray for me."

FLIP IT: "How are you doing?"

- If for some reason you don't have your broken record memorized –do it now. When you are in the car alone, practice saying your broken record over and over.

- Write out and memorize your broken record. You will be prepared.

- Take it in baby steps. Set time limits when you first begin new relationships and new social situations. Always have an exit plan prepared –a reason you must go. Set time limitations for yourself.

My exit plan will be:

Some examples you can borrow from me are:

- I have an early morning, so I need to take off.

- I am expecting an important phone call, so I need to take off.

- I procrastinated on a work project, so I'm going to have to go.

Please try to find the one that is your truth. Lying never turns out well!

My memorized exit plan is:

- Always. Always. Always give yourself grace. If you go somewhere thinking you were ready for it and you change your mind, give yourself grace and go home. It is not a failure; it is a readiness issue. Grace-to-self. Always.

Dear Hikers,

Remember fellow hikers. Most people are cheering you on and are thinking the very best of you. They are just thrilled that you showed up. Think of it as baby steps. Stop by for a short period. Take all the pressure off and give yourself grace when you feel you need to take off. This will not always be your situation; however, it is your situation today. Baby steps all the way!

MC xoxo

It's time to self assess.

Where are you today on Grief Mountain?

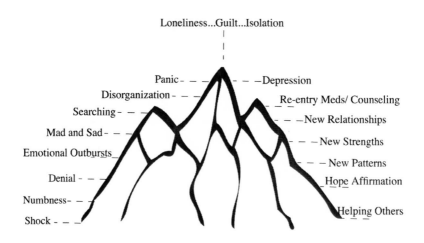

Loneliness...Guilt...Isolation

Panic - — — — Depression

Disorganization - — Re-entry Meds/ Counseling

Searching - — — — New Relationships

Mad and Sad - — New Strengths

Emotional Outbursts — New Patterns

Denial - — Hope Affirmation

Numbness - — Helping Others

Shock - — —

CHAPTER 9

New Life and New Liberty

I want to start off with a very important point. The new adventure is the place on the hike where you have been working really, really hard and you're tired and drained and you see the sign on the trail that says, "Scenic View." And as you make your way to see the view you think to yourself: "It was all worth it." You feel liberated and energized and for the first time you experience that feeling that says, "I am going to be okay." It is at this place where a strange "survivors' guilt" or strange shame can show up. Its unexpected, unfamiliar and unwanted. You feel bad for feeling good. You feel like you are abandoning the person/situation by feeling better. Please let me interrupt this thinking for you. The reason you are no longer stuck on Grief Mountain is because you have done the work required to get up and over it. The result is increased peace, healing and happiness. Release yourself from second guessing your new happiness or energy. It is the goal. The person or the situation you are grieving would want you to arrive at this place. Their greatest desire is for you to be happy and to move on. So, do just that. Embrace your new energy and accept your newfound happiness and power forward.

Be prepared for some temporary back slides. You can find yourself in the new adventure stage and then wake up one day or hear a song that reminds you of the person/situation and now you have slid down the mountain to Emotional Outburst. In the most unexpected place you are rushing to the bathroom stall so you can have a good cry. That is the maddening part of this journey. Don't panic. Don't think you are never going to get better. It's just a temporary back slide. Give yourself grace and let it happen. Use your exit plan if you need to. When you are ready to go back up the mountain, shore up your tools and get back on the trail. The hike begins to shift at this point of the journey. In the beginning, grief has a fog, a thick, dense, never ending barrier between you and the world you once knew. At one point you figured it would lift, as fog does, but after days and weeks spent bundled up you begin to wonder if the fog becomes a part of your everyday life. You so badly want to feel normal, yet the simplicity of normal existence seems unfathomable. Impossible. Then one day you look over your shoulder and see a lot of Grief Mountain behind you. And when you snap your head back forward, the future has color and growth ahead. The tears come a little less and laughter comes a little more. The nights are a little more restful. The smallest sliver of light cuts into the dark and you realize that this must be what healing from grief looks like. The goal is to communicate with your grief as though it has its own personality. You will talk to your grief and you will listen to your grief. Your self-talk might sound like: "Well, Grief! We made it." Or, "I see you there, Grief." Or, "Not now, Grief!"

Grief is funny, you know. You desperately want it to go away and then you also don't want it to go away. Over the course of time and the trip up Grief Mountain, it seems, love has gotten all mixed up with pain and grief. You fear that if the pain eases, then your love for the lost one is leaving you too. These feelings are oh-so-common. I promise. It is common to feel extremely conflicted about feeling better. And although it may not seem rational, it is common to gravitate towards the pain. It is there where it feels like the alternative to feeling pain is losing connection to your loved one. What other choice do you have? So, what do you do?

In your journal make three critical 'Note-to-self' entries

Note-to-Self #1

Remember, your loved one's memory does not live in the pain of your grief. Your loved one's memory remains and lives in YOU. It lives in the stories that you tell. It lives in the things you do, and it has breathed in every silly little thing you do to stay connected to them.

Note-to-Self #2

Embrace the idea as pain diminishes that you may actually find more space to continue bonds and to keep your loved one's memory alive. As pain evaporates, you have more energy and mental space for new things.

Note-to-Self #3

Settle it in your soul to continue bonds. Your connection to the loved one became part of your daily connection. Even as you move forward with your new normal, you may be surprised at how you can create new traditions and bonds to your lost one.

As we stand on the lower base of the Grief Mountain, we find ourselves trying to define what "moving on" looks like. It feels so weird and cringy to say it. That phrase "moving on" is common in the grief/loss world but it isn't very well understood or, frankly, all that helpful. What does moving on mean? What does moving forward look like? How does a person really do it? Unfortunately, there isn't a clear answer to those questions. However, what I have learned personally and professionally with other hikers is that there are helpful things to know about moving on after a death or loss, divorce or other painful life events.

There are four critical mindsets to take on at this point.

1. We are not responsible for how others feel about our grief process. Typically, it feels like what those around us mean by moving on is for us to stop hurting, stop talking, stop crying and just stop grieving. They talk and wish we would stop dwelling on the hurt and encourage us to accept what happened.

   • The truth is what they want is for us to stop making them uncomfortable. It is difficult to watch someone grieve. I get that. However, other people's discomfort with your grief is their issue, not yours. You are not responsible for their comfort.

2. Moving on doesn't mean forgetting. It feels like we get messages from those around us that in moving on, we must forget. That's not what moving on means. Moving on means more about learning to live what I call the "both/and" life rather than "either/or." It's not about grieving or forgetting or being sad, nor is it black and white. Grief lives in the gray.

3. Moving on doesn't mean the end of Grief Mountain. Moving on from grief doesn't mean a static end. It doesn't mean we're suddenly done grieving and will never hurt again. Moving on is more about moving forward than being done. Grief and loss are complex, multifaceted and multilayered. They are both integrated into our lives moving forward. We get stronger as we carry them. They don't simply disappear. Grief can and will continually remind us of our loss in different ways and at different times.

4. In due time, you get to define "moving on" for yourself. People will have all kinds of advice and well-meaning intentions about how you should move on, when you should be done and what it should look like. They, however, cannot determine that for you.

There are no timelines, rules or regulations to the grief hike. You will move through it at your unique pace and not a minute faster. The progression of grieving is unique to each of us. No amount of pressure from others can make us move through our process any faster, not in any kind of healthy way.

Only you know when you are ready to move forward after your loss. Only you decide what it means to let go and accept the loss you experienced. Only you can truly decide what it means to move forward. Whatever it looks like for you, it is perfect and powerful.

Grow Strong Strategies:

1. At the top of your sheet of paper, draw a line down the middle of the page. Label the left side with My Normal Life. Make a list of all the routines and traditions (prior to the loss) that were a part of your life.

   My Normal Life   Possible New Routines/Traditions

2. Take a red pen and write where the barriers are in this transition for you.

3. This might be a good time to write a letter to Grief and say "so long." Probably not goodbye because Grief will bubble up from time to time. However, you could say so long and let Grief know you are moving on.

   • How do I feel about writing a letter to Grief?

4. Grief is not only a door closer; it is a door opener.

   • Journal about doors that you see opening now:

5. Negative beliefs about grief will lead you to a dead end. Be aware of these and cut them loose from your belief system. They will make you a permanent resident on Grief Mountain rather than a traveler hiking up and over.

Be aware of these negative statements/myths and shake them off:

- You never recover from a loss of death.

- Time alone will heal grief.

- If you love someone too much, your grief will be worse.

- Nobody else can help you with your grief.

- The death of a spouse is more painful than divorce.

- A slow death is easier to handle than a sudden death.

- If you just keep busy, your grief will go away.

- It must have been God's plan. (It's never Gods plan to cause you pain.)

NONE OF THESE ARE TRUE STATEMENTS. Shake these off as fast as possible.

- Journal on how these make you feel and if you have ever held these in your belief system.

- What is your new belief system about grief?

It's time to self assess.

Where are you today on Grief Mountain?

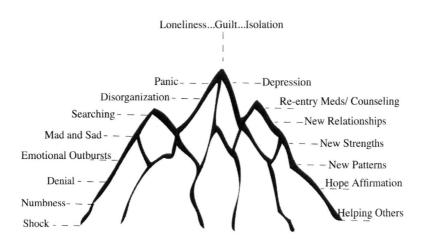

Loneliness...Guilt...Isolation

Panic – – – – – – Depression
Disorganization – – – Re-entry Meds/ Counseling
Searching – – – – – New Relationships
Mad and Sad – – – – – New Strengths
Emotional Outbursts – – – New Patterns
Denial – – Hope Affirmation
Numbness – – Helping Others
Shock – – –

CHAPTER 10

You are now the Trail Guide

Because we have conquered Grief Mountain, we are able to help others. We are back on the ground looking over our shoulder at the mountain as we move forward. Once we have moved into our own healing, we have healing to give away to someone else. We really can't help others while we are hiking over the mountain. It is often in this moment that our test becomes our testimony. The tragic loss is now our mission. We have come full circle and into a place of believing that maybe this all happened so that we could help fellow hikers along their journey. If you have ever been lost in the dark and you see someone coming with a flashlight toward you, you experience relief like no other! You thank God that someone is heading your way with a light to direct you back to the right path. You are now the Trail Guide for Grief Mountain. You can share your story, offer a word of encouragement or hand them this book. Your story will bring them hope that they too can make it over the mountain.

As any good hiker knows, at the end of the climb you will have lots of sore muscles to repair. This is the time to celebrate your accomplishment and plan something very special for yourself. Grief Mountain is a hike that we may go up and over a few times in our life, but for now you need to breathe, relax, rest and celebrate your progress.

I want to give you a careful warning that grief will bubble up now and again. This will happen at different times of the year –anniversaries, events, holidays, etc. You will spot it and say, "There it is." Maybe you will slide back down the mountain to mad & sad. You might go see your coach/counselor and do some journaling. And then, you pull up your boots and keep going.

Remember, as new adventures and new relationships develop, that this is part of the healthy recovery and a result of all your hard work. There is a reason you are doing well. There is a reason you are in this place. You decided to read this book and do the work. Grief only gets better by making the journey over Grief Mountain. Have you ever met someone who has experienced a tragedy and they are changed forever? People make comments like, "They are just not the same person anymore." Sadly, these are people who will not put their hiking boots on and start their journey over Grief Mountain. Grief is so intense that if it goes unattended it has the potential to paralyze you and keep you stuck forever. I know that sounds harsh but I have seen it firsthand. I have been an eyewitness to the emotionally and socially paralyzed person. That is not God Almighty's best for you. Don't guilt yourself with inner dialogs like: "I should not be this happy." "People will wonder why I am doing so well." "I really should be sadder." I believe the reason we go through trials is to equip us to help other people. My greatest trials are my greatest qualifiers in working with people. The very trial is what allows me to connect on a deep level with other people. When you have experienced a loss or tragedy, your well runs deep and you have a deep reservoir to emotionally connect with others. This grief, at one time, made you cringe, avoid or deny. Now it becomes an entity in your life that makes you transparent and approachable for others.

Much like physical shape, staying in grief shape means practicing your tools and staying on top of your new habits; these continue to move you forward. Like anything else, if you consistently use your tools, they become habits and those habits become a lifestyle. It is important to think about the people in your life who need you; they need you to be healthy and engaged. Remembering that you are needed is a tremendous motivator. Sometimes if we are struggling with moving on, it is other people that keep us going. And that's okay.

I cannot stress enough the importance of self-care. I want to shout it from the top of Grief Mountain! Self-care is an absolute must in staying in grief shape. I have noticed over the years that when self-care begins to take a back seat in daily life, it gives room for the grief to sneak back in. For some reason these go hand in hand. Low self-care brings mad & sad back to life. It is also important when we discuss staying in grief shape that you carefully pick and choose what is the healthiest way for you to keep the loss in your life without having it tip you over. I had a client who would go to the grave-yard and visit her loved one every day. This became such a detriment to her everyday life. It took so much energy to recover from her sadness each day. She decided to stop going daily and just visit on special occasions. As you make these types of decisions, you want to find that healthy balance between what will bring you comfort and what is going to set you backwards. This balance is critical to staying in grief shape.

Another element to managing your grief is to "give yourself permission" to move forward. There will be some weird moments where guilt will pop up. You may feel guilty about being happy again or exploring new things. In these moments, be aware of your self-talk and remind yourself of the difficult mountain you have just hiked. Remind yourself of the grit and the hard work that you have put in to making it over Grief Mountain. This is exactly where you want to be; this is the goal. So, turn up the positive self-talk, give yourself a pep talk and enjoy where you are and where you are headed. The people around you, who truly care for you, are cheering you on. Grief Mountain is a taxing brutal hike to summit. Grief is not meant to ever be a permanent place to live. It is a destination, a journey to be traveled. Remember as you are moving forward in life with your people, opportunities and new places that this is how the meadows feel when you are off the mountain. You see the beautiful mountain flowers and feel the warmth of the sun. Take a moment to breath in your progress. Whisper to yourself: "You're doing this!" And maybe even an: "I'm proud of you." I know I am proud of you. Of us.

Grow Strong Strategies:

1. Be prepared for the sneaker wave. In all honesty, grief/loss will be with us all of our life. It is like that cup of hot chocolate! You dump it out in the sink and there is usually some chocolate clinging to the side and the bottom of the cup. There is just a little residue remaining. Grief will have a little residue as well. You string together many good days, yet you can still get knocked over by the sneaker wave of grief. It knocks you over in the most unexpected times. Be prepared for the sneaker wave and don't panic. Just identify the grief, process it, journal it and stay on your journey.

Have you had the sneaker wave hit you yet?

- Reflect and journal:

2. Get in front of your calendar. In dealing with grief it is important to get out in front of your calendar and make some plans to deal with anniversary dates, holidays, traditions and special dates that involved your loss. Carefully go through your calendar and decide what you want to keep the same and what you want to do differently.

- What are my plans for special dates that will trigger my grief?

3. Pace yourself. I believe one of the biggest setbacks on Grief Mountain is when people try to move forward too fast. This hike is paced, and it is important to avoid shortcuts because it will interfere with your healing. In addition, it is important to not get stuck in one place on Grief Mountain either. If you feel like you have been in one phase for a really long time, re-evaluate what is stopping you from taking your next step forward on Grief Mountain.

- Journal and reflect on specific actions or behaviors that are blocking you from the next phase:

4. It is at this point in the journey where our self-care can slide. We are feeling better, so we tend to slack off on our self-care.

   • Journal on new and creative ways to get your self-care in this week:

5. Be aware of your self-talk. Make sure you are acknowledging your growth and your progress.

   • Journal on your three biggest areas of growth and your three biggest progress moments:

6. Be on the lookout for people to share Grief Mountain with. Look into leading a grief group and giving back to someone who is terrified to take the hike. Take a small group through this book. Your hiking expertise is invaluable, and somebody out there needs a Trail Guide. Are you ready?

Dear Fellow Hikers,

You have made it up and over Grief Mountain. You are big, bold and brave to make this hike! And the best news is that the next time grief/loss may strike, you will strap up your hiking boots and you will know what to do. You will summit the mountain again. Grief is a universal human experience. No one escapes grief/loss. Nobody. I want to thank you for letting me be your Trail Guide over Grief Mountain. It has been an honor and a privilege to travel with you.

MC xoxo

It's time to self assess.

Where are you today on Grief Mountain?

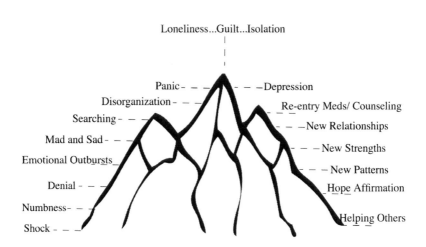

Loneliness...Guilt...Isolation

Panic - — — - — —Depression

Disorganization - — —

Re-entry Meds/ Counseling

Searching - —

- — —New Relationships

Mad and Sad - —

- — — New Strengths

Emotional Outbursts

- — — New Patterns

Denial - — —

Hope Affirmation

Numbness- —

Helping Others

Shock - — —

ACKNOWLEDGEMENTS

Throughout my entire career I have wanted to give a loud huge shout out to the many bold and brave people that I have traveled with over Grief Mountain. I have watched transformation after transformation and their fingerprints are all over this book. I have been an eyewitness to the deep, depths of despair and to the fresh wind of a new beginning. My first and most important acknowledgement is to my private practice peeps. They inspire me every day.

I want to thank God for giving me the vision for Grief Mountain. When I was in graduate school, we were studying the stages of grief and I saw it as a mountain –and God revealed the rest! As a fellow traveler I have ventured over this mountain many times and will continue to for the rest of my life.

I want to thank my parents for their endless love for me no matter what or where I am in life. They continually show up and pick me up. I have been blessed beyond all words by my parents, Marilyn and Dwight Cranston. I am who I am because they are who they are.

I want to thank my son, Walker, for his gentle spirit and mercy that so easily flows from him. I know God gave him to me as a son, but now he is one of my closest friends. Walker has witnessed the despair of my grief and has loved me through it. Whew, I'm so blessed.

I am overwhelmed with gratitude for my best friend, Cyndi Pollard. Cyndi makes me better. She brings me up higher. She challenges me deeply, loves me unconditionally and she reminds me of my worthiness. And every-day I see Jesus in her.

I am so grateful to Joel Boyer. Joel has mad creativity and I am so blessed to have him as my book cover designer. God created Joel to think and cultivate outside the box and I am blessed by his heart and boldness to stay in the creative lane.

I have been hugely blessed by my graphic artist, Sophia Teft. Sophia is one of the smartest and hardest working human beings I have ever met. Sophia is such a gift to me with her beautiful smile and can-do attitude.

I want to say a huge thank you to Dennis Pollard. When I was in the low of the lowest lows Dennis was there for me. He showed me protection and love when I needed it the most. Without a shadow of a doubt, Dennis Pollard is always there for me.

I want to deeply thank my administrative assistant, Melanie Boyer. Melanie is right there and keeps me on task! I love being in Melanie's presence because of her depth and courage.

I am extremely appreciative of my son, Weston. Weston is one of the most insightful and discerning people I know. He started as my high energy, on the go, little boy and transitioned into this confident Godly assertive man. I love being in his presence. He makes me bolder and better.

Afterthoughts

The story behind the story! I am a daughter of a Hall of Fame Coach dad and a mom who navigated her way through the 1970's Women's Rights Movement. My mom was a part of the first generation of women to move from traditional roles to women's equality. She was among the first generation of Super Mom's who were doing it all –home and career. I know her navigation through this momentous movement has had a trickle-down effect on me as a girl. So, you can imagine how I was raised and how my belief system was created. My life tagline is: Nothing Changes if Nothing Changes. I am a *can-do, find a way, toughen up, seize the day, no time like now, if it is to be - it is up to me,* Coach

John Wooden *pyramid of success, where there's a will there's a way* –type of girl. That's me.

And then I met grief. And none of those philosophies worked. Not one. Trying to toughen up would land me in a corner crying somewhere. What had consistently worked before all of a sudden did not work. The grief journey was like no other journey I knew. It was long, taxing and miserable. Nothing in my family, background, education or profession could have prepared me for grief. Honestly, for the first time in my life, I came face to face with something bigger than me.

My first serious personal experience with grief came when I ended my basketball career. I had dedicated myself in every aspect of my life for this sport and now it was over. I didn't know who I was without basketball. I was so uncomfortable in my own skin. I had lost my identity and was mourning something I loved like no other. Grief created a season of mild depression; I was living a life of avoidance.

My next experience with grief had to do with multiple moves and relocations. This felt like whiplash on every corner. It seemed like every time I got settled, we were moving again. Grief created a wall between me and other people –keeping them an arms distance. I was protecting myself. This became my norm.

And of most recent, I experienced divorce after 30 years of marriage and three adult children. What? No one in my family is divorced –like five generations back. That's not what we do, yet, here I am, a Christian coach, author and speaker. I can say it was for the best, but if I had not actively pursued my hike over Grief Mountain I would have been lost to shame, depression and isolation.

Grief Mountain was created solely and selfishly for my own survival. Every aspect of this book is carved out of my personal practices and application. Firsthand. Personally. And to be honest, I would not be who I am or where I am without Grief Mountain. So that is purely my intention in writing this book. If you find yourself in the pain of an identity loss, personal crisis, a divorce, or any other kind of grief, duck and take cover because it has the potential to take you out! Combat grief by reading, studying and applying this book until you cross over this mountain. I did it. You can do it too!

The story behind the story is that Grief Mountain with God at the helm has saved my life. Over and over. It is an epic and universal hike.

MC XOXO